Getting Creative:

Developing Creative

Habits that Work

Drew Kimble

CONTENTS

Part II
Putting Your Creativity into Practice

PLAN. FAIL. REPEAT.

It's 5:30 on a cold Tuesday morning in February.

Your alarm clock goes off, but you stay motionless under your comforter, hoping that it will turn itself off. Last night you promised that you would get up and go to the gym before work, but all you can think about right now is staying wrapped up in your warm cocoon and getting another 45 minutes of sleep.

Or maybe it's 9:00 in the evening. You just put the kids down to bed, and the house is finally quiet. Earlier you promised yourself that you would work on that new painting, or finish that next chapter in your novel, but now you're too exhausted to even think about doing anything productive. Before you know it, you find yourself lying on the couch with a big bag of chips and the television remote in your hand.

What's wrong with us?!

Why is it that some people can jump out of bed first thing in the morning and some of us can't? How exactly does anyone have the time and energy to work on their creative projects after coming home from a full day of work and putting their kids to bed?

Is it because they have more time or energy than the rest of us? Or is it the fact they were simply born with more self-discipline and motivation?

Maybe they stumbled upon some secret organizational system that not only gives them the opportunity, but also the energy to create their art. Or maybe this is all just a bunch of crap that we tell ourselves in order to make us feel better.

Why can't we do the stuff we want to do?

How can we say that we want to do something day after day and still not do it? Is it because it's too difficult, it takes too much time, or is it simply the fact that most of us have the willpower and self-discipline of a fruit fly?

After all, we are always forcing ourselves to do stuff that we don't want to do, whether it's doing ab-crunches, flossing our teeth, or eating Brussels sprouts. So why can't we get ourselves to do the things that we say we want to do?

Is it because we don't have enough time, energy, or motivation? Or is it something else? Why would getting ourselves to do something we want to do, be any more difficult than doing all of the crap we don't want to do?

So how do we follow through? How do we find the time and energy to do the things that are most important to us?

Maybe the first step would be to admit that what we're currently doing doesn't seem to be working.

PASSION IS A TRAP

"Inspiration is for amateurs, the rest of us just show up and get to work."
~Chuck Close

We've all heard the sayings...

"Love what you do."
"Follow your passion."
"Enthusiasm is the fuel that drives your dreams."

However if there is one thing I've learned about creativity and getting stuff done, it's the fact that it doesn't really matter how you feel—it's what you do.

Despite what you may have heard, passion has never painted a picture or written a single word. Feelings come and go, which is why we can't rely on them to fuel our creative goals.

Creativity is not always exciting

When we first start creating our art, we are filled with all of this excitement and enthusiasm. We can't wait to start painting, writing, or taking pictures of everything we see. This is our creative honeymoon period where everything is awesome and each day is a brand new adventure.

Then one day it suddenly becomes work.

A deadline comes up, a commission falls through, or a rejection letter shows up in the mail. Suddenly it starts to feel a lot more like work, and it's not as much fun anymore. Our initial enthusiasm begins to fade, and we start looking for our next grand life adventure.

Passion vs. Consistency

Let's face it, nobody becomes a writer because they love the process of writing—they may love the idea of writing. But the actual process or writing is often frustrating, boring, and a hell of a lot of work.

Sure we want to become writers because we like writing (or, at least, the idea of writing) and we become artists because we like painting and creating beautiful things. Like any other job, however, there will always be good days and not-so-good days along the way.

There's a reason that the tortoise wins the race. In the long run, consistency will beat passion and excitement every single time.

Passion burns itself out, and excitement eventually fades away, but consistency is all about putting our head down and doing the work whether we feel like it or not.

Even though we may not be able to control how our audience will respond to our creative work, the one thing we can always control is the amount of work we are willing to do.

Passion and motivation are unreliable

Don't get me wrong, there's nothing inherently wrong with being excited about your project or getting yourself psyched up to achieve your dreams. Having enthusiasm for your project is great, but unfortunately, it is also extremely unreliable.

Enthusiasm comes and goes because it's based on things like our mood, the people around us, and how we might be feeling that day. This is the reason why so many New Year's Resolutions fail. We expect our enthusiasm to last and be enough to carry us through the tough times—but it never does.

We can't create motivation on demand

Because our motivation is based on our constantly changing emotions, we can't really create enthusiasm in ourselves any more than we can demand love from someone else.

As ironic as it seems, it's very difficult to change the way you feel simply by wanting to change the way you feel. In other words, we can't simply overpower our emotions with reason and logic because it just doesn't work that way. Our feelings can change without warning, which is why our enthusiasm often abandons us when we may need it the most.

Motivation is kind of like that unreliable friend who is fun to have around, but always seems to disappear when you need something from him. This is why we can't count on being motivated when it's time to sit down and do our creative work.

We overestimate our ability to do stuff

We have also fooled ourselves into believing that if we simply have enough enthusiasm and desire, we'll be able to exercise more, eat less, and create a better life for ourselves. So we come up with all of these big goals, and we give it everything we have—only to end up failing again and again.

It's not so much that we can't do these things, it's the fact that we often go about it the wrong way. We end up fighting against ourselves, which is a battle we can never hope to win.

We blame our abilities but not our methods

Why is it that we're so quick to blame ourselves and assume that we don't have what it takes to achieve our goals, when perhaps what we need to do, is rethink our strategy. What if instead of constantly struggling with our emotions, we could find a way to use them to our advantage?

Maybe it's time that we approach things from a slightly different perspective...

HABITS AREN'T FREAKING MAGIC

"Forget inspiration. Habit is more dependable. Habit will sustain you whether you're inspired or not. Habit will help you finish and polish your stories. Inspiration won't. Habit is persistence in practice."
~Octavia Butler

These days it seems like everyone is talking about habits.

Everywhere you look there are books and magazine articles promising to teach us about how we can create good habits and destroy bad ones. There are thousands of articles online that reveal the *"12 Habits of Becoming a Better Writer"* or the *"17 Habits of the Most Productive Artists"* But what exactly are habits and what can they really do for us?

Habits are little-automated routines (both good and bad) that we've accumulated throughout our life. We have habits that we do when we first wake up in the morning and throughout the rest of the day.

We live most of our life on auto-pilot

Some of these habits are simple routines, like brushing our teeth or making our morning coffee, while other habits like driving ourselves to work, can be slightly more complicated. Either way, we often don't even notice when we are doing them because these habits have become such an automated routine in our daily life. In fact, one research study at Duke University found that more than 40% of the actions we perform each day are not conscious decisions at all, but simply automated habits.

For better or for worse, habits allow us to run on autopilot for a good portion of our day. This way we don't have to micro-manage our daily life. Our habits automatically take care of our more routine tasks, which allows our conscious brain to focus on the things that require our immediate attention.

Habits work because they remove the thinking part of our brain (i.e. excuse making factory) from the equation. In other words, we don't have to weigh the pros and cons every time we decide to get a cup of coffee, brush our teeth, or make our breakfast—we just do it automatically.

Then again, habits aren't freaking magic

Habits are only established routines, which means they can't do the work for you. It's like buying a cookbook full of healthy recipes—if you don't actually cook the food, it's probably not going to do you much good.

After all, I would think that most of us know how to do a sit-up, but knowing isn't enough. We need to find a way to turn this information into action. In other words, coming up with big ambitious goals is great, but finding a way to actually do them is even better.

GETTING STARTED SUCKS

"Let's face it, writing is hell. I get a fine warm feeling when I'm
doing well, but that pleasure is pretty much negated by
*the pain of getting started each day." ~*William Styron

Getting started is often the hardest part

Once we start moving, we're usually okay, but for most of us, it's the getting moving part that's so difficult. Whether we are talking about getting out of bed in the morning, going to the gym, or sitting down to work on our novel—getting started is hard.

Anyone who goes running first thing in the morning knows that getting out of bed is often the hardest part. When that alarm clock goes off, your brain immediately shifts into excuse-mode:

"It's too dark."
"It's too cold."
"I don't have enough time."
"I need more sleep."
"I feel like I'm getting sick."
"I've got too much other stuff to do."

Let's face it, there are plenty of good reasons not to get out of bed in the morning and go for a run. Over the years, I think I have dealt with most of them, which is the reason I no longer have a habit of running in the morning. Instead, I've developed the habit of just getting myself dressed and going outside.

In fact, I've given myself permission not to run.

I've made a deal with myself that all I have to do is get up, get dressed, and then go outside—that's it. Once I'm outside, I can either decide to go for a run, or go back into the house and make a cup of coffee.

Of course, most days I end up going for a run since I'm already up and moving, but I'll admit there have been more than a few days when I've gone back in the house to do something else. Either way, I did what I was supposed to do: I got up, got myself dressed, and went outside.

Every time I completed this routine, I succeeded whether I actually went for a run or not. I eventually figured out that it wasn't really the idea of running that my brain had been fighting so hard against, but the idea of getting out of my warm, comfortable bed. So instead of trying to motivate myself to get up out of bed and go for a three-mile run, I changed my goal to simply getting up and getting myself out the door.

Some people might say that I just lowered the bar, and maybe that's true. Then again, I've discovered that I am far more likely to make it over a bar that I can easily step over, than one I may have to jump in order to clear.

Simple goals aren't just for losers & slackers

Later on, I used this same type of "low-goal" technique for my writing as well.

In the past I had set up ambitious word count goals or minimum time limits to create a daily writing habit as all of the experts had told me to do, only to find myself back on that never-ending treadmill of failure and frustration.

One day I might write 1,200 words and feel like crap because I fell short of my 2,000 daily word goal. Another day I may only have time to write for 20 minutes and would end up skipping it because I knew that I wouldn't have enough time to reach my daily writing goal of 90 minutes.

Instead of inspiring and motivating me, all that these "big" goals ever did was make me miserable, because I felt like I was always on the verge of failing (again).

All talk and no action

We all have that one friend or relative who is always talking about their next big goal and how they plan to change the world. Whenever you see them, they are full of passion and excitement, but six months later when you run into them again, they have already moved on to something else—a new exercise plan, a new diet, or some foolproof plan for making money. They have all of these big ideas, but for whatever reason they just can't seem to follow through with anything.

In my experience, saying that I want to do something and then not doing it, is often worse than not setting any goals in the first place. It's not only unproductive, but going through this cycle of failure over and over again has a way of destroying your self-confidence.

The real problem, I suspect, is not so much that we are incapable of achieving our goals, but how we choose to go about it.

Big goals = Big resistance

How many times have you come up with some ridiculously big goal for yourself only to later become completely overwhelmed by it and give up? If you're anything like me, you have probably done this to yourself more times than you would like to remember.

So why do we do keep doing this over and over again?

Don't get the wrong idea here. There's nothing inherently wrong with "dreaming big" and coming up with life-changing goals for yourself. In fact, I would encourage you to do so. The problem for most of us, however, is not that we come up with all of these big ideas, it's the fact that we don't do anything about them.

11

Run like hell (and then collapse)

Most of us are all-or-nothing when it comes to working on our goals. We are either putting in ridiculous amounts of time and energy trying to do everything at once, or we're doing absolutely nothing and trying not to think about it.

We tend to work on our life goals in short highly-motivated sprints. We run like hell until we finally exhaust ourselves, and when we discover that we haven't come as far as we thought we would, we just give up and decide to do something else.

At the beginning of a new project we are usually so full of excitement that we can't wait to get started, so we dive in head first. We do this not only to make up for lost time, but it's also a lot more fun because it feels like we're going to somehow reach our goal faster. So we give it everything we've got—more hours, more effort, more of everything.

Instead of working out for 1 hour a day, we go for 3 hours. Instead of just eating healthier, we decide that we'll consume nothing but some green colon cleansing crap that we read about in a magazine. Instead of writing for 30 minutes a day, we decide that we're going to complete our first novel in 30 days.

Then we beat ourselves up when it doesn't work out.

What's holding us back?

So what's the problem? Why can't we just stick with something and see it through?

I think there are several reasons that we fail to achieve the goals we set for ourselves and it's not because we don't have enough time, energy, or talent.

1.) We think it's going to be too difficult, and we'll fail.
What if we don't have the right education or the right skills to do what we want to do? What if it's too difficult and we can't figure it out. What's the point in trying if we're going to put in all of this time only to get hopelessly stuck along the way?

2.) We think it's going to take too much time and effort

Maybe we want to write a novel, but we can't face the fact that it might take us a year or more to do it. Maybe we want to go back to art or music school, but we know that it's going to take a lot of time and money. Or maybe we want to lose 20 pounds, but we don't want to give up our free time to go to the gym.

3.) We think it's going to hurt (our body, mind, or pride)

We hate that feeling of pain and awkwardness, which is why we do everything we can to avoid it at all costs. One of the first questions we ask ourselves before we attempt to do something is, Is this going to hurt or make me look like a complete idiot? If the answer is, yes, we'll probably do everything we can to keep ourselves from doing it, especially if it's something we don't have to do.

Lowering our expectations

What if we've got it all wrong?

What if we're really not as weak-willed, lazy, and pathetic as we fear. What if the problem is not so much with ourselves or our abilities, but with the flawed strategy we've been using?

Maybe what we need to do is lower our expectations a bit. Not necessarily about what we can accomplish, but how we go about it.

Instead of trying to force ourselves to write 2,000 words a day and continually falling short, maybe we need to find a way to break down our goals into smaller bite-sized pieces that we can more easily accomplish. After all, you can create dozens of goals for yourself, but if you can't get yourself to work on any of them, then what's the point?

Usually, it's that first step, simply getting the ball rolling that takes the most effort.

Again it's not the actual running that's so hard; it's getting out of bed first thing in the morning that makes it so difficult. So maybe it's time that we change the way we think. Instead of trying so hard to finish our goals, maybe we need to focus more on finding ways to help us get started and put our habits into motion.

Drew Kimble

FINDING OUR CREATIVE TRIGGERS

"You can, you should, and if you're brave enough to start, you will."
~Stephen King

There's no fire without a spark

Before you can write 2,000 words a day, you have to be able to sit down and write a single sentence.

Before you can paint your masterpiece, you have to find a way to pick up your paintbrush.

Before you can accomplish whatever it is you want to achieve, you need to find a way to take that first step.

Why having a trigger is so important

A trigger is something that sets off your routine.

I like the idea of a "trigger" because it reminds me of one of those classic Rube Goldberg mechanical contraptions, where a single movement puts everything else into motion. For example, if I'm going to take our dog for a walk, I'll grab her leash, and she immediately knows that she's going for a walk because that's her trigger: leash = walk

Even though our lovable chocolate lab isn't necessarily the brightest pup on the block, she knows exactly what's going to happen from the moment I pick up her leash. First we go for a walk, then a long drink, and finally, a biscuit that she will eat curled up on her bed. That's the routine, and as far as she's concerned, it's as inevitable as night following day.

Dog trainers use this triggering process all the time using voice commands, hand signals, or the "clicker". The big secret here is that this process works just as well for people as it does for dogs.

Buzz —> Click

"An object at rest stays at rest, and an object in motion stays in motion."
~Isaac Newton

If it's true that once you start a routine, you will tend to keep going, then the trick is to find a way to get started.

Think about some of the different habits and routines that you are already doing every day and then try to find that first step (or trigger) in the process. What specifically do you do that sets everything else in motion?

For example, when I am going for a run, I'll get dressed and put on my running shoes (which I only wear for running) which signal my brain to get into running mode. Or if I'm going to free write, I'll pull out my journal and my favorite pen, which shifts me into writing mode. Similar to showing my dog her leash, these things have become signals to my brain about what is going to happen next.

Connecting triggers to a creative habit

So how do you associate a trigger with a particular action?

Usually, the easiest way to do this is to find a way to associate a trigger with an already existing habit. So if you listen to a particular type of music every time you get your paints out and work, the chances are that music has already become an unconscious creative trigger for you. Once you recognize this, there are certain things that you can do to strengthen this trigger.

For example, you will want to have the shortest path possible between the initial trigger and your creative act in order for your brain to more easily make the connection.

$$A \longrightarrow D$$

is a stronger trigger than

$$A \longrightarrow B \longrightarrow C \longrightarrow D$$

In other words, if you turn on your "creating music" and then brew a cup of tea, check your emails, and update Facebook before actually painting anything—your music trigger is going to be a lot weaker than if you simply turned on the music and got to work. We'll talk more about this idea of immediacy along with a few additional ways that you can strengthen your creative triggers in an upcoming chapter.

Focus on your trigger, not the creative activity

This idea goes back to what we talked about earlier, which is setting the bar low enough that you don't become overwhelmed and start making excuses.

What you don't want to do is to think about having to sit down and write 2,000 words before 10:00 a.m. Instead, you just need to focus on getting the creative process started before you have the chance to talk yourself out of it.

Just one sentence.

Just one brushstroke.

And then go from there.

Triggers don't have to be something you do

Keep in mind that there are many different types of triggers that you can use other than physical actions. Things such as changing your creative environment, time of day, and location can also function as creative triggers. We're going to talk more about how you can get these different types of triggers to work together in the next chapter.

Drew Kimble

MANAGING YOUR
CREATIVE ENVIRONMENT

"My concern at times is nothing more than establishing a series of practical considerations that will enable me to work. For years I said if I could only find a comfortable chair, I would rival Mozart."
~Morton Feldman

Setting up your creative environment

One of the things that many creative artists underestimate is the importance of establishing a supportive, creative space and how much it can affect their overall productivity.

For whatever reason, we tend to think that creativity is all inside our head. We don't realize how much our environment can significantly affect our mood and our ability to create. However, if we aren't able to find a way to control our work environment, location, and any other potential distractions—we will end up fighting a losing battle.

We like to do what's easy

Let's face it, nine times out of ten we eat unhealthy crap because it's easy and the most convenient. We stop at fast food restaurants for breakfast and lunch because they are quick and cheap. We order pizza or carryout for dinner because we don't have the time or energy to cook anything else.

If every time we want to sit down and do our creative work, we need to first clean off our desks or pick up our studio, chances are, we're going to find a way to avoid doing it. This is why it's important that we make the process of sitting down to create, as easy as possible.

Human nature tells us that if we want to do anything consistently, we have to make it as painless to do as possible. So if your goal is to eat better, you need to have healthy food available that is just as convenient to eat as the packaged crap in your cupboard. Likewise, if you want to sit down and do your creative thing every day, you are going to need to set up and control your environment just as carefully.

Don't surf where you work

However, it's not just about making things as easy as possible. Creating strong triggers and habits is just as much about consistency and exclusivity.

This means that we not only need to follow the same routine consistently to form a lasting habit, but we should also keep our creative space exclusively for our creative work. In other words, you shouldn't use your writer's journal to create to-do lists, and you shouldn't use your painting studio as your junk room.

Keep in mind that I use the word "studio" loosely because there seems to be this perception out there, that if you don't have some fancy dedicated room to do your creative thing, you can't consider yourself to be a real artist or writer. This, of course, is just another excuse for not doing anything.

Now having said that you should try to find some type of dedicated space that your brain can learn to associate with your creative work. Again this doesn't have to be anything fancy. Pretty much any location will do as long as you use it consistently and exclusively for your creative work. It doesn't matter if it's an unfinished basement, a closet, or a folding card table sitting in the corner—as long as whenever you are in that particular space, your brain knows that it's time to sit down and get to work.

This is all part of training your brain and establishing your creative triggers. When you go to your workspace, you should automatically associate it with your creative work.

It's like when I pull out the leash to take our dog for a walk. She knows exactly what it means because we don't get her leash out when it's time for her to eat or go to sleep. We use it exclusively for walks, so the moment she sees it, her little doggy brain automatically shifts into walk mode. We also use the leash consistently, which means that we don't try to mix things up and pull out her stuffed monkey when it's time to go for a walk. It's the same leash and the same trigger each and every time.

Over the years, we have trained her by being consistent and exclusive with the routine and the tools that we use. And even though our human brains may function at a slightly higher level than my adorable but dim-witted Labrador retriever, the habit-forming process is exactly the same. We need to be consistent and exclusive with every creative trigger that we use.

Not one size fits all

In the next few chapters, we're going to be talking about some of the creative habits, routines, and triggers that have worked for many different writers and artists, but that doesn't necessarily mean that all of them will work for you. Everyone is different, so you'll just have to experiment to see what works and doesn't work for you personally. The best place to start is usually by looking at what you are already doing.

What I suggest is that the next time you are having a productive day, take a minute to write down exactly what you did immediately before and during your creative session:

What did you do before you got started?
What time of day was it?
What did you eat or drink before getting to work?
Do you go anywhere or do anything different than usual?
Did you do any type of physical activity beforehand?

And then while you were working...
Where were you?
Were you listening to music or was it quiet?
Did you notice anything different or unusual around you?

21

If it doesn't work, try, try again... wait, what?!

Just by answering these types of questions, you can often find clues about what types of triggers and habits work best for you—even if they are not what you expect or hope them to be. For example, I love the idea of writing with music playing in the background, but over the years, I've discovered that it just doesn't work for me.

Part of the reason I wanted this working with music thing to work is the fact that I really enjoy listening to music. I also figured that writing while listening to music would help to feed my creative muse. After all, the author Stephen King is well known for writing with heavy metal music blasting in the background. So if he does it, it must be a good thing, right?

Well, not necessarily.

The problem was that even though I enjoyed it, I never seemed to have a good writing day when I had the music playing in the background. Even though I could tell that it wasn't helping me to write, I really wanted it to work so I just kept on trying day after day.

I listened to everything from rock to blues, to cheesy 80's movie soundtracks—but I would always find myself listening to the music instead of putting words on paper. Eventually, I had to face the reality that the music was distracting me and cutting into my productivity, so I forced myself to stop.

My point here is that you need to take the time to experiment and find out what actually works for you, and not simply do what you enjoy or works for other creative artists you admire.

TIMING IS EVERYTHING

"I write when the spirit moves me, and the spirit moves me every day."
~William Faulkner

Planning to be creative

I used to think that all I needed was to find a stray 30-40 minutes out of my day where I could sit down and write. And most days I was able to find at least a little bit of time here and there. Sometimes it was after work. Sometimes it was in the evening after the kids went to bed while other days it was first thing in the morning.

The problem, of course, is the fact that creativity isn't a switch that you can turn on and off at random moments throughout the day. Sitting down to write isn't like throwing in a load of laundry or checking your email, where if you have a few spare minutes, you are still able to get something accomplished.

The truth is, you need to plan for creativity.

All time is not created equal

It's not just about finding some spare time during the day to create; it's also about finding time to work when you are at your most creative. Keep in mind that this may not necessarily be the time of day you would like it to be.

I know because I really wanted to be one of those people who could pop up out of bed at 4:30 in the morning, grab a cup of coffee and start writing. This schedule not only worked out better for myself and my family but after doing a little research, I discovered that it had worked for a lot of other famous artists and writers as well.

The only problem with this plan was the fact that I kept waking up day after day with gibberish on the screen and drool on my keyboard. So as much as I wanted to be an early-morning writer, it just didn't work for me no matter how many times I tried.

Some people are just naturally more alert and creative in the morning while others find themselves to be more creatively inspired late at night. One is not necessarily better than the other. The trick is to find out what works best for you, and then find a way to make it happen.

"Back in the day, when my kids were little...
I had a schedule so regular that it was practically Pavlovian,
and I loved it. The school bus came, I started to write.
The school bus returned, I stopped." ~Francine Prose

What if you're not available during your "creative time"?

Maybe you'll discover that you do your best painting or writing at a time when you are either working or dealing with the kids. What are you supposed to do?

Finding that delicate balance between doing your creative work while still handling your family responsibilities is not always easy. It can become even more difficult if your peak creative time doesn't naturally sync with your work or family's schedule. Unfortunately, there are no easy answers, but here are a few strategies that might be worth trying.

If you have young kids at home, you might consider getting to bed a little earlier and then waking up in the morning before they do. On the other hand, if you are the type of person who works better at night, you might try staying up a little later and then asking your spouse to get the kids breakfast in the morning. Or if your work schedule just doesn't fit with your creative schedule, maybe you could schedule a block of time over the weekend and enjoy a mini creative retreat. Even if none of these options are ideal, you have to find a way work with what little time you have available and understand that it won't always be like this.

At the same time, don't allow yourself to fall into the trap of seeing your creative work as an all-or-nothing kind of activity. Far too many artists and writers I talk with have essentially put their creativity on hold until their life slows down, their work schedule changes, or their kids leave home. Before they know it, they wake up and realize that it's been ten years since they have picked up a paintbrush or written a word in their novel.

Something is always better than nothing. If you only have 20 minutes to write or paint during the day, sit down and find a way to use it rather than telling yourself that it's not enough time.

In the end, creativity is a habit like flossing your teeth—you either do it, or you just talk about doing it. Sure it would be great if we all had the time and resources to do whatever we wanted to do, but that's rarely the way life operates, so we just have to do what we can with what we've got.

Why do so many creative artists work in the morning?

"I am not very bright or very witty or very inventive after the sun goes down." ~Toni Morrison

Even though there are plenty of visual artists and writers who like to work late into the night, there are many more who prefer to do their creative work first thing in the morning.

For many people waking up at 5 or 6 o'clock in the morning may be the only opportunity they have to sit down and create due to their family or work schedules. Others just like the quiet and solitude the morning offers them before the frantic daily rush of activity begins. Many of them also believe that their mind is far less cluttered first thing in the morning, which allows them to focus better on their creative activity.

Now having said that, it's still not for everyone.

Since I'm already up by 5:30 a.m. during the school year,

getting up even earlier than that and expecting to function just doesn't work for me—but I also know a lot of writers and visual artists who swear by their early morning creative sessions. So if you're one of those people, here are some tips to get you started.

Start slowly

Begin by getting up just 30 minutes earlier. You can't just wake up 90 minutes earlier one day and expect to function. You have to start slowly and work into the new schedule gradually. Like pretty much anything else, consistency here is the key. Make it a point to get up at the same time for at least a week and then actually go to bed when you are tired. If your plan is to stay up late and still try to get up early, you are probably setting yourself up for failure. Unless you're a college student or someone who can grab a quick nap in the middle of the day, you probably can't have it both ways.

Make it as easy as possible

Program the coffee maker the night before and make sure the thermostat is set to warm up the house by the time you are scheduled to get up. Trust me, it's tough to crawl out of a warm bed at 5:00 a.m. when you are facing the prospect of sitting alone in a cold room with no coffee in sight.

Have all of your supplies ready to go.

The last thing you need after crawling out of bed is to spend 20 minutes of your creative time looking for your writing journal or the paint brush you were planning to use. Get everything ready to go the night before so you'll be able to sit down and get to work as quickly as possible.

Don't get distracted along the way.

Once you are up and have grabbed your favorite hot beverage, go directly to your studio or writing area. Resist the urge to check your email, Facebook status, Twitter updates, and see what you missed while you were sleeping. There will be plenty of time to catch up with the rest of the world later. This is your creative time, so use it.

Time of day can also be a creative trigger

Whether you decide to have your creative time first thing in the morning, in the middle of the day, or long after everyone else in the house has gone to bed, your brain will eventually begin to anticipate and shift into creative mode around this time as long as you are consistent.

Find what time of day works best for you, and then stick with it. Make a schedule for yourself and then honor that commitment. Let the other people in your life know that this is your creative time and they shouldn't interrupt you unless it's an emergency. This goes not only for your kids but also for your spouse, relatives, and roommates as well. This shows them that this creative time is important to you, and chances are they will support you as long as they see you taking it seriously.

You don't need 8 hours a day to be a creative artist

This is probably one of the biggest complaints I hear from people every day. They simply don't have as much time as they would like to dedicate to their art. I understand that, but here's the thing, I'm pretty sure that nobody feels like they have enough time to do what they want to do.

Then again even if we did, we probably couldn't handle it anyway. Because nobody can be creative 8 hours a day, every day.

Stephen King, the author of over 65 books only writes 4-5 hours a day. The prolific composer Igor Stravinsky believed that three hours of focused composition was about the most he could handle in a single day. Anthony Trollope managed to write 47 novels but rarely wrote for more than 3-4 hours a day. Trollope himself once said that *"...three hours a day will produce as much as a man ought to write. But then, he should so have trained himself that he shall be able to work continuously during those three hours."*

The writer and philosopher Jean-Paul Sartre agreed with this idea of working in short creative bursts. "One can be very fertile without having to work too much. Three hours in the morning, three hours in the evening. This is my only rule."

Keep in mind that these are just examples and are not a secret recipe for creative success. There is nothing magical about working for three hours a day. It's just that because of the level of focus and concentration that creativity requires, most of us can only work for a few hours a day before we are completely drained both mentally and emotionally.

While there are certainly those rare exceptions, even those who are full-time writers typically split up their day between creative composition and more routine tasks such as editing, proofreading, or research.

Finding your best time to create is only the first step

Once you have discovered the best time of day for you to create and have worked it into your daily schedule, you can further strengthen this creative trigger by adding some additional cues such as managing your location, eliminating distractions, and establishing small creative rituals—which are some of the things that we'll be talking about in the following chapters.

LOCATION, LOCATION, LOCATION

There is a time and place for everything

When I was growing up, this was one of my parents favorite things to say when I was caught doing something stupid. They wouldn't usually tell me what I was doing was wrong, but they would say that it wasn't appropriate for that particular time or place. Even to this day, I'm not sure if this was a result of enlightened parenting, or if it was just their way to get me to stop acting like an idiot out in public.

This isn't unusual because most of us associate certain types of behavior with specific locations. That is, we tend to behave differently in a fancy restaurant with our in-laws then we would in a sports bar with our friends. In other words, our location (as well as our companions) often determine what is, and is not, acceptable behavior.

As creative artists, our location can not only affect our behavior, but it can significantly impact our mood and level of productivity as well. This is why we need to do what we can to control our creative environment, including where and how we choose to work.

Consistency and exclusivity are the key

Most of us could benefit from having a specific place for us to do our creative work.

As I said before, this doesn't necessarily have to be anything fancy. It can be a dedicated room in your house, but it can also be a folding table in the corner of the basement or a booth at your local coffee house. The important thing here is that whatever location you choose, you should only use it when you are creating.

This type of exclusivity will help you to eventually associate that particular location with your creative work. From the moment you walk into this location, you will begin to automatically shift into creative work mode. It's just like when you walk into your gym; your brain begins to prepare itself for your upcoming workout. The location becomes a trigger for the activity.

This is why you shouldn't "share" your creative space with other activities. As soon as you start watching TV or checking your email in that same location, you begin to weaken that creative trigger. Instead, you want to do everything you can to strengthen that connection between location and activity.

From the moment you sit down, everything you do should be telling your brain that it's time to get to work and create something.

What to do if you don't have a creative space at home?

I'll be honest, I tried for years (unsuccessfully) to fight this type of location trigger. I had convinced myself that I could write on the same computer that I used to check email, pay bills, post updates on Twitter, shop online, listen to music, and watch funny cat videos on YouTube. I fooled myself into thinking that I somehow had the self-discipline to ignore all of that other stuff when it came time to sit down and write... which of course I didn't.

What would usually happen, is that I would sit down and write a few paragraphs and then suddenly remember that I had to email so-and-so, or I'd be curious what my friends were up to online and switch over to Facebook and Twitter, or maybe see if Amazon finally put that DVD set I've been wanting on sale. It became an endless series of just-one-more-thing until finally my creative time was up and I realized that I had only managed to write 150 words. Instead of writer's block, I was dealing with a severe case of WDS (writer's distraction syndrome).

We'll be talking more about dealing with these types of distractions in the next chapter, but for now, we are going to be focusing on how we can use our location as a way to boost our creative productivity.

Just in case you are curious about how I dealt with this computer distraction issue, I eventually broke down and purchased an old IBM laptop for about fifty bucks and disabled the wireless card. Then when it was time for me to write, I would pack it up and head down to the local library.

There was no web browser, no apps, and no music on the computer—it was just me pounding away on some creaky old version of Word running Windows XP. My options were essentially to either write or stare at the wall. When my time was up, I would save whatever I was working on to a USB drive so I could transfer it later to my home computer for formatting.

Every time I stepped into that library and headed towards that same claustrophobic cubicle in the corner, my brain began to automatically shift into writing mode. The bonus was that I didn't have to worry about someone stealing my crappy laptop if I left it unattended.

Don't get me wrong, writing wasn't any easier.

Unfortunately, there wasn't any magic writing dust sprinkled in that particular cubicle and some days I would just sit there and stare at the screen wondering what the hell I was thinking trying to write anything at all. The most important thing, however, was not how much I wrote or how easily the words were flowing on that day, it was the fact that I wasn't doing anything else. For better or for worse, I was there to write.

Finding your creative space

Your creative studio might be a separate room, a corner of your basement, or it might be a cubicle at your local library or coffee shop. Keep in mind that it's really not about what kind of space you have, but what you do when you're there. Again, consistency and exclusivity are the keys here. So do whatever you can to find a space, create a routine, and then get to work.

Sometimes a change of scenery is inspiring

Although it's true that consistency and exclusivity are important to your productivity, it is still possible to fall into a rut by following the same routine day after day.

When this happens, many writers and artists have discovered that simply by changing things up a bit, they can refresh their creative imagination. The director Woody Allen often noticed this particular trait in himself, and whenever he found himself stalling out, he would immediately force himself to change his location.

"I've found over the years that any momentary change stimulates a fresh burst of mental energy. So if I'm in this room and then I go into the other room, it helps me. If I go outside to the street, it's a huge help... It breaks up everything and relaxes me."

I have found this to be true myself, which is why if the weather is nice, I'll sometimes leave my windowless library cubicle and head to the local park with my laptop. And even though it may not turn out to be the most productive writing session, simply having that change of scenery almost always brings me a new perspective or a renewed sense of energy for my project.

MANAGING DISTRACTIONS

Let's face it, managing distractions is a big part of the creative process.

Even though everyone is different and nobody reacts to particular distraction the same way, we're going to take a closer look at some of the most common distractions out there and see if they might be hurting your creative productivity.

So how do you know if something is a distraction?

Generally speaking, if you consciously notice something around you when you should be working, it might be a distraction. It might be the background music playing, a noise outside, a ping from your cell phone, or it could be that big pile of papers and miscellaneous crap sitting next to you on the desk. Again, what's distracting to one person, may not bother someone else, which is why you just have to experiment and see what type of things tend to distract you the most.

Clearing the clutter

I know that some people are bothered by clutter and can't seem to focus if their surrounding work area is messy. I'm not one of those people, but maybe you are. I lived with a bunch of guys in college, so I've built up a fairly high immunity to crap and clutter (just ask my wife), so it doesn't really seem to affect me one way or another, but I know for a lot of people it can become a distraction.

So I would simply experiment and see how your productivity is affected when your work area is cleaned up and organized versus when it's not.

At the same time, I would caution you not to let your preference for tidiness interfere with your creative time. I've seen writers and visual artists who normally hate the idea of cleaning anything, turn into rabid cleaning machines if it means they can avoid sitting down and doing their work.

So if you want to clean up your workspace before or after your creative work time, that's great, just don't clean when you should be busy creating.

Clearing your mental space

It's not always enough, however, just to tidy up your desk or clean out your studio. You may need to clean out some of your mental space as well.

As I mentioned, physical clutter has never really bothered me, but mental clutter has been known to stop my creative productivity dead in its tracks.

From the moment I wake up, I start putting together all of these elaborate to-do lists in my head. In fact, before I've even finished my first bowl of Lucky Charms, I've usually come up with dozens of things that I need to remember to do that day.

The temptation here, of course, is to start working on all of these other projects and get them out of the way before I sit down to write. The only problem is that I never actually finish my to-do list, or by the time I do, I'm so exhausted that the last thing I want to do is sit down and write.

Mind dump

This is one of the reasons I usually start any creative writing with a 5-10 minute free writing session either on the computer or in a paper journal. Typically this is not related to anything I'm going to be working on. Usually, it's more of a random thought repository and a quasi to-do list. Whatever information I end up writing down doesn't really matter. What's important is that I'm able to get it out of my head and onto the paper.

Especially first thing in the morning, I've learned that I need some way to empty out all of the questions, ideas, and "don't forget" stuff that has built up in my brain overnight. Once I'm able to get all of this random stuff down on paper, I can usually let it go, which opens up that mental space for creativity.

Then when I'm writing, if I suddenly remember something that I need to do, I'll quickly jot it down, so it doesn't keep bouncing around in my brain, and I can get back to what I'm supposed to be doing.

The power of music

Earlier we talked about working with background music and how it can affect your creative process. Again, everyone is different, and I know a lot of visual artists and writers who love to work while listening to music.

I know I do. The only problem, as I mentioned earlier, is the fact that I can't seem to actually get any writing done while I'm listening to music. So for me personally, I decided that listening to music while I was writing wasn't worth the trade-off. However, that doesn't mean that it's not the right choice for you.

Different strokes for different folks

So are some types of music really better for working than others? Is it true that some kinds of music can hurt your productivity while others may actually help it?

A lot of visual artists and writers seem to do just fine with any type of music while others have found that they prefer instrumental only music while working. Some like to sing along and feel the beat while others just enjoy having some background noise.

One example of this is the American painter Chuck Close, who likes to have the TV or radio playing in the background while he is working. *"I like a certain amount of distraction. It keeps me from being anxious. It keeps things at a little bit more of an arm's length."*

Others prefer to listen to their music before they start to work as a type of a pre-game warmup. The writer William Styron would often play his favorite music for an hour or so before he began his daily writing *"in order to feel exalted enough to face the act of composition."*

In other words, there's not a right or wrong answer here. You really just have to experiment and see what types of music (if any) works best for you. Keep in mind, however that this doesn't mean that you should choose the option that you enjoy the most, but the one that allows you to be the most productive.

It's not just music that can distract you

Although I rarely listen to music anymore when I am writing, I almost always have my headphones on when I'm working outside of the house.

Depending on where I'm at, there always seems to be music playing, babies crying, or people having obnoxiously loud conversations. Most of the time I can block out this type of background noise, but some days it just becomes too distracting.

This is when I fire up Spotify and pull up a "Nature Noise" playlist where I can use the sound of ocean waves or a rainstorm as white noise to block out the obnoxious guy next to me who insists on shouting into his cell phone.

Here are a few ideas to get you started as you conduct your music productivity experiment. These are roughly sorted in order from (potentially) the most distracting to the least distracting types of music.

- Some of your favorite songs you know by heart
- New music in your favorite genre
- Music in unfamiliar genre (not what you usually listen to)
- Instrumental music: Jazz, Classical, Movie Soundtracks
- Nature Sounds: ocean waves, rain, forest sounds, etc...
- White Noise

Under similar working conditions, you may want to experiment by playing these different types of music in the background for a week or two and see how much your creative productivity changes.

Dealing with online distractions

"I write whenever I am able, for a few days or a week or a month if I can get the time. I sneak away to the country and work on a computer that's not connected to the internet and count on the world to go away long enough for me to get a few words down on paper, whenever and however I can." ~Francine Prose

One of the biggest complaints I hear from visual artists and writers these days is about dealing with online distractions, which can mean anything from handling email, impulsively checking social media sites like Twitter and Facebook, to shopping for the latest deals on Amazon.

I completely understand, because as I mentioned before, I seriously suck at self-control when it comes to checking my email or seeing what's happening online when I'm supposed to be writing.

At the same time, I understand that not everyone has the willpower of a fruit-fly, and maybe you don't have a problem dealing with online distractions. If that's the case, feel free to skip ahead to the next chapter. However for the rest of us, I'm going to share with you a few of the strategies that I use in order to save me from myself.

Fighting my online demons

Whether it's me obsessively checking my email, exploring my favorite websites, or getting sucked into some ridiculous YouTube video—I'll be the first to admit that I'm not so great at ignoring the siren call of the internet. I've learned that if I have some form of online access, sooner or later I'll find myself neck deep in Twitter updates and adorable kitten videos.

Using the internet kill switch

They say that the first step towards wisdom is to "know yourself". Well, I've been around myself long enough to know that if I have internet access, chances are I'm going to find a reason to use it. Usually, it starts innocently enough in the name of research, but it's never too long before things start to spiral down the internet rabbit hole.

Sadly it's come down to me having to completely disable my internet access when I'm supposed to be writing. I've already mentioned my hobbled laptop solution for those times when I'm working away from home, but when I'm writing at home, the online world becomes a much bigger temptation.

I know what you're probably thinking... why don't I just use the same laptop when I'm at home? Well honestly I have, but I've also found that it's a lot harder to use the clunky laptop when my shiny iMac is sitting right there in front of me with all of my writing and formatting apps ready to go.

At some point, I decided to compromise, and now I simply turn off my wi-fi connection when I'm supposed to be writing. That way there is no email, no browsers, and no status updates—it's just me, my keyboard, and my embarrassing lack of self-control.

Again, turning off the computer's wi-fi connection is what works for me. Other writers and graphic artists I have talked with have used time management apps to disable or severely restrict their internet access for a certain period of time.

Although finding a suitable location and dealing with potential distractions are two of the biggest obstacles that keep us from doing our work, there are a few additional things that we can do to help keep the creativity flowing.

RITUALS AND ROUTINES

"Serious writers write, inspired or not. Over time they discover that routine is a better friend than inspiration." ~Ralph Keyes

Finding your own creative rhythm

Once we have setup our creative space, we can further strengthen our creative habits by establishing some rituals and routines that will help to support our daily practice.

The power of routines and rituals

I used to think that routines and rituals were two different words that essentially described the same type of activity. Although these words are closely related, I discovered they are also different in some fairly significant ways.

Routines are like habits that we often do unconsciously. Things such as checking our cell phone first thing in the morning. Brushing our teeth, making breakfast, and driving to work are all things that we don't consciously focus our attention on doing. Once we start one of these routines, the automated process simply takes over.

Some of the creative triggers that we've already talked about, such as time of day and location, can become automatic routines if we are consistent with them. However, we can strengthen our daily practice even more by establishing a few "pre-game" creative rituals.

Rituals are a specific type of activity that we do to prepare ourselves mentally for an upcoming task. For example, many athletes use some sort of pre-game ritual to get themselves ready to play. Rituals aren't just for multi-million dollar athletes, however, and many writers and artists have found them to be useful in their daily practice as well.

Sleep experts tell us that following a consistent nighttime routine before going to bed will help us to get a good night's sleep. Some of these activities, like brushing your teeth, might be considered an unconscious habit, while other activities such as reading a book, meditating, or listening to soft music are mental rituals that can also help to clear our mind and prepare ourselves to sleep.

Too often we ignore these more subtle mental rituals and instead focus all of our energy on the larger logistical issues such as finding the time and place to do our creative work. However, we shouldn't underestimate the effect these small rituals can have when it comes to preparing our mind for our creative work. It can be something as simple as lighting a candle, reading a favorite poem, brewing a cup of tea, or listening to a particular type of music before we start our creative work.

These small rituals can not only help to shift us into a more creative mode, but they also remind us that our creative work is something that we should enjoy. In our obsession with time management and maximizing our productivity, we sometimes forget that although creativity requires a lot of hard work and self-discipline, it should also bring us joy.

This doesn't mean, however, that you should be filling your day with a bunch of elaborate rituals that you need to obsessively do in order to function. The goal here is not to create more hoops to jump through before getting to work. These are simply small acts that can help nurture your creative soul.

Mixing things up to keep it interesting

Keep in mind that just like any other habit that we continue to do day after day, we might need to change things up once in awhile in order to keep ourselves on track.

While most of us like the comfort and familiarity that comes from following an established routine, it is possible to become bored doing the same thing day after day. The author Nicholson Baker admits that *"there's something to just the excitement of coming up with a slightly different routine."*

It's kind of like when you are starting a new project and you're filled with all of this nervous energy. While beginnings can often be scary, they can also bring with them a renewed sense of anticipation and excitement for your creative work.

So don't ever feel like you are trapped with a particular habit or routine. You should always feel free to experiment and mix things up along the way. Sticking with your creative practice doesn't mean that you are required to follow the same exact routine forever.

Whether it's the time of day, your location, or the little things you do along the way—you need to always keep experimenting and discovering what works best for you.

CREATIVITY IN MOTION

*"I keep to this routine every day without variation. The repetition
itself becomes the important thing; it's a form of mesmerism.
I mesmerize myself to reach a deeper state of mind."*
~Haruki Murakami

Physical movement as a creative trigger

Don't worry, I'm not going to be lecturing you on how you should be exercising more instead of sitting on your couch binge-watching your way through your Netflix queue. However having said that, when we study the lives and habits of some of the most productive artists and writers, there does seem to be a connection between physical exercise and creative productivity.

In fact in a 2014 study done at Stanford University, researchers found that when people were walking they were 60% more creative in completing certain tasks than when they were sitting. What's interesting is that it didn't matter whether they were walking outside on a mountain trail or walking on a treadmill, the results were the same.

The composers Richard Strauss, Pyotr Tchaikovsky, and Igor Stravinsky were all known to take brisk walks before sitting down to work. On the other hand, Beethoven, Charles Dickens, and Kierkegaard preferred to take their long rambling walks in the afternoon after doing their creative work in the morning. The painter Joan Miró would often paint in the morning and then put on his boxing gloves and spar in the afternoon or take a run.

All of these writers, composers, and artists understood that there is a connection between physical movement and creativity. It turns out that the mind is not as independent of the body as some of us would like to believe, and the condition of one, can directly affect the other.

Creativity in motion

Many creative artists prefer to do some type of physical activity before they sit down to work in order to get the blood flowing and settle their fidgety muscles that can often develop when sitting for a long period of time.

I know that I'm like this, which is why I always try to get up and do something active before I sit down to write. Whether it's running, taking a bike ride, or taking the dog for a walk—I've found that doing something active beforehand not only settles me down physically, but it has a way of calming my mind as well.

Other creative artists, I have talked with prefer to do their creating first and then unwind by exercising afterwards, which allows their subconscious mind to work on the things that came up during their creative session. Again, everyone is going to be different, so it's up to you to experiment and see what type of physical activity works out best for you.

Allowing you mind to wander

Of course, almost any type of activity is better than doing nothing, but when it comes to boosting your creative productivity, all physical activities are not created equal.

Keep in mind that we're not trying to build our muscles or burn the maximum number of calories with any of these activities. In fact, with the possible exception of Miró and his boxing gloves, most writers and artists historically have focused on simple activities such as walking or running to clear their mind.

The reason that we want to focus on these type of simple activities is that we are trying to tire out the muscles and free the mind at the same time. This means that we don't want to do something that demands a great deal of mental involvement. Ideally, what we want is an activity that allows our mind to wander, digest new ideas, and make new connections.

SENSING CREATIVITY

How many times have you heard an old song on the radio and you were immediately taken back to a particular time or place in your past? Or perhaps you've walked into a building and smelled something that reminded you of someone you know?

These are examples of sense memories that go beyond our eyes and often involve certain sounds, smells, or even tastes that we associate with a particular time or event in our past.

Just as we can have a trigger for a certain time of day or location that we associate with our creativity, we can use our other senses as well to strengthen and reinforce our creative practice.

Hey, I remember that song!

It's well known that music can significantly alter our mood. Certain songs from our past can instantly trigger memories and take us back to a particular time or event in our life.

There are songs that were popular back when I was in high school and college that still remind me of a specific event or group of friends. Even though I may have listened to these songs many times since then, for whatever reason, I still associate these songs with that period of my life.

What's even more remarkable, is the fact these are accidental triggers. In other words, I never intentionally tried to make the connection between a particular song and an event from my childhood—it just happened naturally.

Even though some of these connections happened unconsciously, it is also possible to make these type of connections through deliberate repetition, which is similar to forming any other kind of habit. Just like professional athletes who listen to the same playlist before every game to motivate and get themselves "in the zone", you can create your own music playlist to help inspire you before your creative session.

What's that smell?

Have you ever entered a restaurant or someone else's home and smelled something that reminded you of a certain place or someone from your past?

Outside of the scented candle industry, it seems that using smells as a creative and emotional trigger has been overlooked. However, what would happen if we put a particular type of scented candle in our creative space (and only in our creative space)?

Eventually, we would begin to associate that particular smell with our creative work. The smell of that particular candle would subtly reinforce our creative environment and help to remind us why we are there in the first place.

Tasting success

Many people don't realize just how closely our sense of smell and taste are interrelated and how much of an emotional effect they can have on us.

For example, I know one writer who keeps a tin of Altoids next to his computer, and every time he begins a writing session, he pops one of these curiously strong peppermints into his mouth. He swears that the smell and taste of these mints help to shift him into creative mode. Even the small ritual of opening the tin every morning and popping a mint into his mouth has become a creative trigger for him.

Other artists, I have talked with, tell me that they always brew themselves a cup of tea or coffee and take it with them into their studio. They say that the smell and taste of it has a way of shifting them into a more creative state.

Then again, it's going to take more than a cup of coffee

Okay let's be honest, sniffing a candle or sipping a cup of tea is not going to instantly transform you into a super-productive creative genius. Likewise, sucking on an Altoid is probably not going to compel you to sit down and write 2,000 words or force you to start that commission that you've been putting off.

These small little rituals and routines are not intended to be some sort of magic formula. They alone don't have the ability to force you to sit down to create something. At the same time, these little triggers can help to enrich your creative space and reinforce your creative practice.

However, just like any of the other creative triggers that we have talked about, consistency and exclusivity are the key. This means that my writer friend who keeps the tin of Altoids next to his computer, only eats those particular mints when he is writing, which is why he has learned to associate that particular smell and taste with his writing practice.

LET'S GET PHYSICAL

We've already talked a lot about using a particular time of day and location as a creative trigger, as well as using supplemental triggers such as sounds, smells, and tastes to support and enrich your creative environment.

As helpful as these types of creative triggers can be, many artists also like to have something a little more substantial in their creative arsenal. Physical items, such as a particular object or piece of clothing, that they have come to associate with their creative work.

One writer I know keeps an old antique typewriter on his desk, not only because it reminds him of all of the great writers who have lived before him, but he's also hoping to invoke some of the magic of the craft itself. He calls the typewriter his personal talisman to attract his creative muse.

He has also filled his writing space with the books and pictures of his favorite writers. He told me that he liked the "physicality" of being surrounded by the books, images, and tools of his writing mentors. I have also met visual artists who have decorated their studio with the works of their favorite artists in order to inspire and feed their creative spirit.

Creative dress code

The types of clothing you choose to wear (or not wear) while working can become a creative trigger for you as well. For some people, their creative uniform may be a suit and tie while, for others, it may be a simple t-shirt and sweatpants. Some people like to be as comfortable as possible when they work while others believe that in order to take their job seriously, they need to dress the part.

You may have a special writing hat or a particular smock that you like to wear in the studio. You might like to fill your workspace with inspirational quotes, poems, prayers, or works of art—or perhaps you prefer the peaceful zen-like serenity of an empty creative space.

Whatever specific items you choose to use (or not use) isn't important. What's important is that you design your workspace into a place where you can actually get some work done.

PART II

PUTTING YOUR CREATIVITY INTO PRACTICE

WHY SETTING GOALS IS NOT THE ANSWER

"It is good to have an end to journey toward;
but it is the journey that matters, in the end."
~Ernest Hemingway

Why dreaming big is often a recipe for disaster

Everything we've talked about so far in this book has been about giving you the tools that will help you to sit down and do your creative work.

However, even after you figure out the right schedule and set up your ideal creative environment, there are still going to be plenty of days when things don't go exactly as planned, which is why it's important to have a system in place that accepts failure along the way.

Setting goals is not the answer

One of the things that frustrated writers and artists tell me all the time is that they are constantly beating themselves up when they fall short of their creative goals. Part of the problem is that they have set themselves up to fail.

For example, how many times have you said something like this to yourself...

I'm going to write 2,000 words a day.
I'm going to publish a new blog post every day.
I'm going to finish a painting every week.

Most of us like to set these kinds of goals for ourselves because they create excitement, passion, and fuel our big dreams. The only problem is that these goals can also create a lot of anger, guilt, frustration, and a severe case of self-loathing.

With goals, we fail until we succeed.

The problem with having big goals like these is the fact that there is no real sense of achievement along the way. In other words, it's difficult to say that you have achieved a goal until you do.

So what happens is that we spend most of our time stuck in this awkward state of working on our goals, but never quite reaching the finish line. We may even feel like we're making some real progress until something comes up and we are forced to stop.

Eventually, it turns into a vicious cycle, where we start something and make progress for a little while, but then we never quite reach the end. Our novel gets abandoned, or the painting we were once so excited about gets stuffed in the basement with the rest of our half-finished masterpieces. When we aren't able to achieve our ultimate goal, we get frustrated and can't help but feel like we've failed... again.

Unfortunately failure is cumulative, and it tends to feed on itself.

Part of the problem is that we spend so much of our time and energy focusing on the finish line, that we end up ignoring the progress we make along the way. We do this because we've been told that's how it works. You set a goal, and you work on it until finally you achieve the goal... or you don't.

We forget, however, that creativity isn't an all-or-nothing type of activity. Creativity feeds on itself and in the end, everything counts. There is no wasted effort, and every minute that we spend doing it makes us a better creative artist.

We also sometimes forget, that there is a very important difference between achieving our creative goals, and doing our creative practice.

CREATIVE GOALS
VS.
CREATIVE PRACTICE

"What you do every day matters more
than what you do once in a while."
~Gretchen Rubin

The difference between a creative practice and a goal?

A creative practice is based on effort, consistency, and your degree of progress. Some examples might include: How many hours did you paint, write, or practice your instrument in the last week? Are you making progress on your current project? Have you been learning or mastering a new skill or technique?

Creative goals, on the other hand, are usually based on results, deadlines, and the opinions of other people. Some examples might be: Was your latest story or article accepted for publication? How many paintings did you sell at the art show? Did you receive a positive critical review on your latest project?

The important thing to notice here is that pretty much everything in the creative practice category is under your control, while most of the things in the goals category are not. Often the frustration, depression and anger that we feel come from trying to control outcomes and results that are not under our control.

Even the goals that may be somewhat under your control (ex. writing 2,000 words a day or completing a new painting every week) do not necessarily reflect your growth as a creative artist. After all, it's really not about typing 2,000 random words and then calling it a day. Writing, or any kind or creative art, is not simply a mechanical process where you put in your daily quota and then check it off your list. That's just not how the creative process works.

There are going to be times when your project will naturally move faster or slower depending on what type of writing you're doing and where you currently are in the writing process. This is why setting a goal like a daily word count is likely to frustrate and discourage you in the long run.

The important thing here is not that we achieve some arbitrary goal, but that we sit down and do our daily practice. In other words, our success should be measured on whether we have practiced our art and not the final result.

We need to shift our perspective

Success doesn't mean writing 2,000 words a day. Success is sitting down to write every day.

Writing a novel is a goal—Writing five days a week is a practice

Finishing a painting every week is a goal—Painting three days a week after putting the kids to bed is a practice

Running a marathon is a goal—Running four times a week is a practice.

When you base your success or failure on your daily creative effort, rather than your output, you can succeed every time you practice your art.

Make it easy to succeed and difficult to fail

Remember the three reasons we talked about earlier that keep us from achieving our goals in the first place:

1.) We think it's going to be too difficult, and we'll fail

When we ditch our goals and focus instead on our creative practice, it becomes much more difficult to fail because our daily practice is based on effort rather than our final results. Instead of constantly dealing with uncertainty and the fear of failure, we can feel a sense of accomplishment just by sitting down and putting in the work.

2.) We think it's going to take too much time and effort

Writing or sketching for 10 minutes a day is something anyone should be able to do successfully. Now is writing for 10 minutes a day going to finish your novel in 30 days? Probably not, but then again writing 10 minutes a day consistently is going to be far more productive in the long run than writing four hours a day for a week or two and then not touching it again for the next six months. Remember our ultimate goal here is not just productivity, but it's also about finding a way to change our behavior and establish our creative habit.

We also have to keep in mind that writing or painting 10 minutes a day is just a starting point. It's the bare minimum that we have to do each day (every other day, three times a week, etc..) to keep our creative momentum going. Some days you may only be able to work for 10 minutes while other days you might end up working for an hour or two. Your job is simply to get started and see where it takes you.

3.) We think it's going to hurt (our body, mind, or pride)

Let's face it, failure hurts. Every time we fail at something, it damages our pride and the faith we have in our abilities. On the other hand, every time we follow through and do what we say we're going to do, we build up a little more self-confidence. This is why we need to make it as easy as possible to succeed by setting up ridiculously easy "low-hurdle" daily goals for ourselves.

When we begin to doubt that we can achieve what we set out to do, whether it's writing a novel in 30 days or losing 30 pounds, we'll often subconsciously sabotage our efforts because we already know how it will end. We would rather just get it over with quickly than let it drag out and subject ourselves to a long series of daily disappointments and self-loathing.

So what makes a good creative practice?

There are a few ways to tell whether you are creating a goal or establishing a creative practice.

First of all a creative practice, unlike a goal, does not have a specific deadline. This is because we are not trying to create a particular end product. With a creative practice, we are focused more on the journey than the final destination.

But what if I want to write a novel, isn't that a goal?

Even though finishing a novel or a painting can be the result of your creative practice, that isn't the practice itself. For example, your creative practice might be to write for 15 minutes a day, five days a week. Now of course if you stick with this creative practice long enough, chances are you're going to end up producing something along the way—and that's great, but that's not what we're focusing on. With a creative practice we are more concerned with the act of doing than we are with how much we've done.

The second criteria for a good creative practice is that it's realistic, and there is some built-in flexibility.

It doesn't matter if we are talking about writing, painting, or going to the gym. If we commit ourselves to doing our practice seven days a week 365 days a year, we are setting ourselves up for failure and frustration.

No matter what we do, there are always going to be days when we get overwhelmed, or we just feel like crap. We need to accept the fact that every day isn't going to be a creative utopia. That's just not how the world works, sometimes things come up, and life gets in the way. This is why I suggest setting up a creative practice that has some flexibility built into it.

For example, if you are single, or you have more free time than you know what to do with, you might be able to commit to doing your creative thing five days a week. On the other hand, if you're working full-time and have three kids at home siphoning off all your time and energy, you may only be able to commit two days a week to your creative practice.

The point here is that it's important to give yourself some wiggle room—so if today falls apart, you can still get back on track tomorrow. As long as you honor your daily or weekly commitment, you will continue to build on your progress and keep moving forward.

Finally, all of the creative triggers that we have talked about in this book are far more useful for daily practice, than they are for big-picture goals. Remember that these triggers are designed to help get you moving and establish your creative routine. By themselves, they are not powerful enough to keep you motivated for six months while you attempt to finish your 75,000-word novel. However, they may be enough to put your butt in the chair and work on it today.

Smaller goals = less pain + more motivation

Think about this for a moment. If your goal is to write a novel in 6 months, you aren't going know if you have succeeded or failed until after those six months are over. On the other hand, if your goal is to sit down and write for twenty minutes first thing in the morning, you'll probably know if you have succeeded or failed by 11:00 a.m. Not only that but if you do your writing practice today, you can also use that sense of accomplishment and momentum to help get you out of bed tomorrow morning.

Now imagine how you are going to feel if you don't finish your novel after giving yourself six months to work on it. You're probably going to feel like you have failed and start beating yourself up for "wasting" the last six months of your life.

The problem is that as the stakes get larger, the potential rewards may get bigger, but so do the consequences of failure.

So what's the big deal about failure?

We all fail at one time or another right, so why not just "shoot for the stars" and have the courage to fail big?

Here's the thing. If you screw up your to-do list today, it's not really that big of a deal to pick yourself up and try again tomorrow. But what if you've spent the last year of your life (or more) writing a novel or trying to land that big gallery show, but for whatever reason it doesn't work out. How many times do you think you are going to be able to simply dust yourself off after something like that, and try again?

Failing big is fine if you're trying to cure cancer

It's one thing to fail over and over again when you are trying to invent the lightbulb or cure a horrible disease—it's another thing when you are spending your time writing a novel or painting a picture.

As creative artists, we often walk that fine line between doing something that is useful to others, and doing something that may only be useful to ourselves. Now I'm not going to sit here and debate the role of the artist in our society and if he or she is an essential part of it. I'm going to assume that because you're sitting here reading these words, you probably feel that creating art, music, and literature is a worthwhile activity.

My point here is not to question the value of the artist in our society, I just want to point out that if you are setting all of these big goals for yourself and then failing repeatedly, you are far more likely to give up trying to write a novel, than you would give up on curing a life-threatening disease.

This is why I suggest setting smaller short-term goals for yourself, where you will not only be able to taste success more often, but it will also give you the confidence and momentum to continue.

Establishing effective creative habits is about doing all of the little things that can help you to sit down and do your creative work. You will find that the effect of these habits is cumulative, and like the creative process itself, it all eventually adds up.

The secret to productivity is to keep moving

Momentum is a powerful tool itself, and as Mr. Newton observed, a body in motion will tend to remain in motion. As we mentioned earlier, getting started is often the hardest part of the process.

Whenever we start a new project, there is usually a good deal of uncertainty and self-doubt that creeps in that prevents us from taking that first step. This is why it's so important to cultivate our creative habits and routines. Our creative practice not only helps us to get started, but it also keeps us moving forward.

Sometimes you just have to go through the motions

"Inspiration exists, but it has to find you working."
~Pablo Picasso

Let's face it, we're not always going to feel like sitting down to write or picking up our paintbrush. There are going to be days when we just aren't feeling it, and everything we do seems like a giant waste of our time and energy. These are the days when you just have to sit down and go through the motions. You put in your time, and if nothing else, you can feel good that you didn't give in to your resistance.

This is why sometimes the best thing we can do, is to pull out our writing journal or sketchbook and just get the pencil moving across the page. Too often we underestimate the power of movement in our creative process. In my own experience I've found that if I can just get my fingers moving on the keyboard, my imagination will eventually catch up.

This is one of the big secrets that no one ever tells you about creativity. You don't always have to be inspired or in the mood to create. Sometimes you just have to show up, put in the work, and be happy that you made the effort.

There will always be reasons not to create, but if you're serious about your art, you have to find a way to do it anyway. The only way that you can build and maintain your creative momentum is through constant repetition and practice. You have to find a way to sit down and do your creative work day after day—even when no one else seems to care.

SOME GROUND RULES FOR A CREATIVE PRACTICE

How much is too much?

One of the questions that people often ask me is, how many creative practices should I be working on at the same time? Unfortunately, there isn't one answer that works best for everyone.

You see most books on creating new habits recommend that we focus on developing one habit at a time. This is generally good advice because it turns out, we have a limited amount of motivation and willpower to make our habits stick. The only problem with this one-habit-at-a-time strategy is that everything else in our life has to go on the back burner until we can get that one habit firmly established.

The other issue is the question of how long it takes for something to become a habit? Some habit gurus claim that it takes 60 days, others say 3-6 months, and some say that depending on the habit, it could take a year or more to firmly develop a new habit. And how exactly do you know when you've arrived? At what point can you confidently say that your new habit is rock-solid and you are ready to move on to something else?

I don't know about you, but I've got a whole boatload of things that I need to work on in my life, not just one or two. Maybe someone whose life is more together than mine can afford to spend 6 months working on one particular habit while putting everything else on the back burner—but I can't. Sure I would love to create a daily writing habit, but I would also like to work on other parts of my life at the same time.

This is where establishing low-hurdle daily practices can be more effective than having one big goal that takes everything that you've got. One of the other benefits is that you don't have to focus all of your attention on one aspect of your life, such as writing while neglecting the other parts of your life that you would like to work on as well (exercising, playing an instrument, learning a new skill, etc...)

The key is not to overwhelm yourself.

Remember that you want to make your daily practices, no matter what part of your life they are addressing, as easy-to-do as possible. This means creating short, low-hurdle activities that you can do virtually anywhere in less than 30 minutes a day.

For example, you may come up with three daily practices such as 10 minutes of writing, 10 crunches or pushups, and reading for at least 10 minutes each day. So in theory, you should be able to get all three of these done in less than 30 minutes throughout the day. Not only that, but you should be able to do any these activities whether you are sitting at home or on the road.

Importance of practice portability

This idea of "portability" wasn't something that occurred to me when I first started creating these types of daily practices for myself.

For example, I learned that practicing the guitar for 10 minutes a day is hard to do when you're out of town and don't have access to a guitar. Likewise, swimming laps or lifting weights becomes much more difficult to do when you are nowhere near the pool or gym.

This doesn't necessarily mean that you can't do these type of activities. It just means that you may want to have an alternative option available to you as well. For example, if you don't have access to a guitar that day, your alternative might be to study music theory or do ear training for 10 minutes instead that day. Or if you don't have access to your laptop where you usually do your daily writing, you could use your tablet, cell phone, or even a good old-fashioned paper notebook.

The point here is that you either need to have portable creative practices, or you need to set up some alternative activities in advance. What you don't want to do, however, is to use your location as an excuse to do nothing.

Bending the rules by staying flexible

In addition to creating daily practices that you can do almost anywhere, you should also plan to build in some flexibility as well. Earlier we talked about some of the dangers of scheduling a creative practice for seven days a week, and how by doing this, you are setting yourself up for failure.

Let's face it, life can get a little crazy sometimes, which is why it's important to build some flexibility into your creative practice. Not just how many days you do your creative practice, but you should also have some time flexibility as well.

For example, creating a daily practice where you will write for 15 minutes is one thing, but planning on writing for 15 minutes by 7:00 a.m. is something else. By doing this, you are limiting your flexibility and making it that much easier to fail.

This is why I usually avoid assigning specific times to do my daily practice (ex. go to the gym at 7:00 p.m.) or establish a time deadline (ex. finish my daily writing by 11:00 a.m.). I usually do whatever I can to keep things as flexible as possible, so that no matter how busy my day gets or how late it becomes, I will still have the opportunity to do my creative practice.

For almost all of my daily practices, the only deadline I have is that I need to have them completed by the time I go to bed. In other words, if I'm not sleeping, there is still time to squeeze in what I need to do even if it's 1:30 in the morning. What this does is take away my excuse to do nothing because I missed the deadline or ran out of time.

These small daily practices are simply starting points

"Inspiration comes and goes; creativity is the result of practice."
~Phil Cousineau

Remember that when you give yourself a daily practice of writing for 15 minutes a day, that is all you're required to do. You sit down, you write for 15 minutes, and then you can feel satisfied (and guilt-free) because you have successfully completed your daily practice. It's that simple.

Don't allow yourself to fall into the trap of constantly having to "do more" than your daily practice. When the ideas are flowing, and everything is falling into place, of course, you should keep on going—but that shouldn't become your expectation.

Keeping your expectations under control

Once you've completed your daily practice, always give yourself permission to stop. Although this might sound a little silly at first, I have seen how this type of thinking can destroy a creative practice. You become trapped by your ever-increasing expectations of what you should be doing, until eventually no matter what you do, it's never enough.

Let me give you a quick example of how this can happen. Let's say that one day I sit down to write for 15 minutes and everything is going great so I decide to keep writing until eventually I come to a stopping point. I look at the clock and notice that I ended up writing for about 40 minutes. So I put my stuff away and congratulate myself for a having a good writing day.

That's great except now the next day, I sit down to do my 15 minutes of daily writing but after 20 minutes I stall out and find myself going nowhere. However instead of wrapping things up and congratulating myself for completing my daily practice, I start beating myself up because the day before I was able to do 40 minutes, and what's the matter with me if I can't manage to do the same thing two days in a row?

The problem is that my expectations have changed.

Even though my official goal may only be 15 minutes. The unwritten expectation in my mind has become that I should, at least, be able to do 40 minutes if I ever want to become a "real" writer. So even though I tell myself that 15 minutes is enough, my expectation is that I should be doing a lot more than that if I ever want to make anything out of myself.

Suddenly, my daily practice has become much more intimidating. Instead of simply having to sit down for 15 minutes each day to write, I have now set up the expectation that anything less than 40-60 minutes a day is unacceptable. Eventually, this new expectation becomes so overwhelming, that it's easier just to give up.

So although it's great to go above and beyond your daily practice, learn to see it as a bonus, and don't ever allow it to become your expectation. It's a subtle difference, but it's also something that can destroy your creative practice if you let it.

Start small and build from there

Anyone who has ever made a New Year's resolution knows that our ambitions can often be larger than our willpower. I remember one year I made the decision that I would get up every morning and do 100 crunches. That particular resolution lasted about four days before both my abs and my motivation fizzled out. Another year, I vowed to write 5,000 words a day (because I had read a book about someone who supposedly does this). Needless to say, that didn't exactly work out for me either.

My point here is that as human beings, we tend to overestimate what we can do. We assume that how we feel today, is how we are going to feel tomorrow, and the next day, and the day after that. Unfortunately, that's not how life works. What excites us and motivates us today, often bores the crap out of us tomorrow. Which is why if you are relying on motivation and passion for achieving your goals, you are likely setting yourself up to fail.

Somedays you are going to be excited to do your creative practice and feel like you can take on the world, while other days you're going to feel like you are just wasting your time and going through the motions. Unfortunately, that's just the way life works.

You don't have to love it; you just have to do it

What really separates those who eventually succeed from those who don't, is not how talented or motivated they are, it's their ability to do their creative work whether they feel like it or not.

I often tell people that it's kind of like brushing your teeth. You don't do it because you enjoy it or because you're so excited about the idea of good oral hygiene—you just put the toothbrush in your mouth and do it. Somewhere along the way you've figured out that it takes more energy to come up with excuses not to do it, than it does to simply stick the toothbrush in your mouth and be done with it.

In fact, that's one of the secrets to creating a good creative practice. It has nothing to do with being excited or motivated about what you're doing; it's just about finding a way to get it done.

It's okay if you don't believe me...

I know that some of you will be tempted to ignore this advice because you think that you aren't as weak-willed as the rest of us—and I get it because I was once like you.

Like I said, I was one of those people who was naturally drawn to setting up big dramatic goals for myself. Doing 100 crunches a day, writing 5,000 words every day, or deciding on a whim to completely eliminate sugar from my diet.

Over the years, I had absorbed the advice of every self-help guru out there who told me that small goals were for small people, and that in order to win big, you had to dream big. My attitude reflected that famous quote by Norman Vincent Peale, who said that we should always, "shoot for the moon" because "even if you miss, you'll land among the stars."

The only problem was that I could never seem to make it to the moon or the stars. Instead, I would find myself crashing back to earth time and time again frustrated and angry at my inability to follow through with anything in my life.

This cycle repeated itself over and over until eventually, I decided that I had to try something else. If dreaming big and setting big goals wasn't working for me, what if I did the opposite and came up with an easier goal instead? Not just easy, but stupid easy—so easy in fact that it would take more energy to come up with an excuse not to do it. That's when I sat down and wrote the following goal on a scrap of paper that I taped to my computer monitor: "Write for 10 minutes a day".

At the time, I didn't really think it through any more than that or set up any additional rules for myself. More than anything, I think I just desperately wanted to prove to myself that I could actually follow through with something—anything.

I knew that I wanted to make writing more of a priority in my life, so I figured this might be one way to make it happen. After all, if I couldn't fit 10 minutes of writing somewhere into my daily schedule, something was clearly wrong either with my life or my priorities.

A couple of things ended up surprising me about this ridiculously small goal of writing for 10 minutes a day. First of all, I began to understand that I didn't really have to write at a specific time or place. I could sit down anytime during the day I had a few extra minutes and just write for ten minutes.

If you're a writer or visual artist yourself, you might understand what a revelation this was for me. After all, I had always been taught (or perhaps simply assumed) that a writer could only write in their sacred writing space at a certain time of day where there were no other distractions.

Secondly, I had always believed that a writer had to be "inspired" in order to write. In other words, you couldn't just sit down after dinner or stop off at a park on your way home from work to do your writing that day. The conditions had to be just right. You had to be in the mood and bursting with creative thoughts and ideas. Otherwise, you would just be wasting your time.

It turns out, however, that none of this was true.

I also assumed that 10 minutes of writing a day wasn't enough to add up to anything. What I didn't realize, because I had never tried it before, was how often I would keep on writing after my time was up. Sure there were those days (and still are) when I'm feeling tired, and as soon as my 10 minutes is up, I shut things down. However, there are also just as many days when I would get on a roll and just keep on going. That's when I began to realize that my issue wasn't so much with writing itself, as it was getting myself to sit down and start writing.

Again, I'm not asking you to believe any of this; I'm just suggesting that you try it out for yourself and see what happens.

SETTING UP YOUR FIRST CREATIVE PRACTICE

"To practice any art, no matter how well or badly,
is a way to make your soul grow. So do it."
~Kurt Vonnegut

Okay, let's say that you are willing to give this whole creative practice thing a try, where exactly should you start?

Even though the last thing I want is for you to overthink this whole process by making it too complicated or giving you a bunch of rules to follow, I do have a few suggestions that might make setting up (and being able to live with) your first creative practice a little easier.

Start with one practice

If you're anything like me, you probably have a long list of things you would like to work on in your life. I get it, but for now in order to keep things simple, we're going to focus on setting up just one creative practice. Later on, if everything goes well, you can always add a few more down the road. By only focusing on one creative practice to begin with, you will significantly reduce the risk of overwhelming yourself.

Make it a ridiculously easy

Remember that you want to make your first creative practice so easy to do that you won't have to rely on self-discipline and willpower to get yourself to do it. Don't forget that one of the goals here is to prove to yourself that you can follow through and do what you say you are going to do.

Here are a few suggestions to keep in mind as you come up with your first creative practice:

Low hurdle: Make sure that your first creative practice is something that sounds ridiculously easy to do. Again, we're not just talking "easy" here, but complete no-brainer I-would-have-to-be-an-idiot-if-I-couldn't-do-that type of easy. Here are a few examples to show you what I'm talking about:

- 10 minutes of writing/painting/instrument practice
- 10 minutes of reading
- 10 pushups or crunches
- 10 minutes of meditation

Time vs. Productivity: Some people have asked me whether it's better to set up your creative practice by the amount of time (e.g. 10 minutes) or the amount of productivity (e.g. write 100 words). My answer, is that it kind of depends on the type of activity (What exactly is 30 seconds of crunches?) and your personal preference. Now having said that, I generally prefer to use time for most of my own creative practices because I can easily set a timer and then not have to think about it, but it really just depends on what works best for you.

Understand why you are doing it: Make sure that your creative practice is really something that you have been wanting to do. This may sound a little ridiculous, but you would be surprised how many people create daily practices for themselves for things they don't want to do. So why do they do it? They do it because it's what they think they should be doing, or maybe it's what other people are doing. If you really want to practice the piano because you love to play, that's great. But if you're just doing it because your Mom forced you to go to piano lessons when you were growing up, don't waste your time or willpower trying to make it happen.

Before you commit to anything, always ask yourself why you would want to spend your valuable time working on this activity.

Once a day: You first creative practice should be something that is only performed once per day. Again, we want to keep things as simple and easy to do as possible.

Your first creative practice should be "portable": Ideally, your creative practice should be something that you can do virtually anywhere. If the creative practice you choose isn't something that's portable (e.g. playing the piano), make sure that you sit down and think about some alternative activities in advance.

Your practice should take less than 15 minutes to do: This is the maximum amount of time from start to finish. Personally, I prefer 10 minutes because it's a nice round number and that amount of time doesn't intimidate me, but I've also talked with people who have used everything from 3 minutes to 15 minutes for their creative practices. You may be tempted to go longer than 15 minutes, but I wouldn't recommend it. Again, this is simply the minimum amount of time you need to do, and you always have the option to keep going for as long as you want.

You have until your head hits the pillow to complete it: Be sure to build some flexibility into your first creative practice by not setting up firm deadlines that require you to race the clock. This not only takes off some of the pressure, but it also eliminates the "it's too late" excuse. In other words, if your daily practice is to sit down a write for 10 minutes and it's 11:30 at night, you will still have the opportunity to do what you need to do.

Do a creative practice test drive

Before you commit yourself to any creative practice, be sure to try it out first and make sure that it's a good fit for you and your current lifestyle. I've talked with more than a few people who have made the mistake of jumping right in only to discover later that something about their creative practice didn't work for them, and they were eventually forced to give it up. You simply won't know if a particular creative practice is going to work for you until you try it out for a week or two.

When in doubt, make it easier

The temptation will always be there to dream big and do more. However if you ever find yourself becoming burned out with your creative practice, the solution is often to do less, not more.

From experience, I can tell you that when I start to feel burned out or completely overwhelmed by the thought of having to do my daily practice, it's usually because I initially set the bar too high.

Your motivation to do your creative practice will naturally come and go. You're not always going to feel like doing it, and that's okay, but at the same time, you should also never feel overwhelmed or dread the idea of having to do your daily work. If this happens, it usually means that you have set your initial expectations a little too high and you may need to adjust things a bit.

But isn't this kind of cheating?

Should we really be allowed to adjust our creative practice as we go along? Isn't it just a matter of summoning up enough self-discipline to push through the low point until things turn around? While this may seem to be a great test of our moral fiber, all that usually happens when we try to fight our way through these rough patches, is that we end up exhausted and defeated.

Remember that doing 5 minutes of writing a day is far better than doing no writing at all. So when you start to feel burned out for more than a day or two, try to find some way to make your daily practice a little easier before you ever reach that point of giving up.

HOLDING YOURSELF ACCOUNTABLE

Many people have heard the stories about how the writer Ernest Hemingway loved to stay out late drinking with his friends. What most people don't know, however, is the fact that even when he was out late drinking, he was still at his writing desk almost every morning by 6:00 a.m. He also had the habit of closely tracking his daily word count on a chart after he finished his writing each day.

Hemingway realized the importance of establishing and sticking with a creative routine. He also understood the power of holding himself accountable by continually tracking his daily progress.

Don't break the chain

There is another famous (and possibly completely made up) story about the comedian Jerry Seinfeld. He said that one of the keys to his eventual success was that he found a way to sit down and write new material for his act every day, even in the beginning when no one else cared.

He created a system for himself where he would hold himself accountable for sitting down and writing every day. What he did was to put one of those big yearly calendars on his wall where he would always see it. Then he would put a big red 'X' across every day that he sat down and worked on his material.

Seinfeld said that "After a few days, you'll have a chain of red X's", and then if you "just keep at it, the chain will grow longer every day. You'll like seeing the chain, especially when you get a few weeks under your belt. Your only job is to not break the chain."

Once you have created a long enough chain, you may discover that you would do almost anything to keep going and not "break the chain." The genius of this system, I think, is in the visual feedback of the calendar. Eventually, it becomes a type of game or contest with yourself. How long can you make it? How many days can you go without breaking the chain?

We create our habits and then our habits create us

The writer Samuel Johnson once said that *"the chains of habit are too weak to be felt until they are too strong to be broken."* He understood that this combination of momentum and pride can be a very powerful force in shaping human behavior.

Although I personally prefer to use a paper calendar because it's right there staring me in the face every day, there are several smartphone apps that can help you to track your daily progress as well. You can find a more detailed list of these type of accountability apps in the free bonus guide to this book.

It's not about making yourself feel guilty.

Tracking your progress and holding yourself accountable is about building momentum and a sense of pride that comes from following through on your commitments. Once you reach a certain point, you realize that you don't want to stop because you see how far you've come.

Keep in mind, however that there's a fine line between motivating yourself and beating yourself up because you stumbled somewhere along the way. So if you do find yourself "breaking the chain" at some point, don't take it personally. You have to understand that it's going to happen sooner or later, and that's okay.

REWARDING YOURSELF

Small rewards create happy habits

Whether it's dealing with my kids or our hyperactive Labrador retriever, I've learned that rewards really do work. I've also learned that bigger rewards are not necessarily better, and that frequent small rewards are often more powerful in shaping our behavior.

So how can we use this information to help us follow through with our creative habits?

Connecting habits with happiness

If our creative triggers are the beginning of our habit loop that sets things in motion, then the reward is our incentive to repeat the cycle and do it all over again.

Trigger —> Creative practice —> Reward

When we give ourselves a small reward for following through with our creative practice, we create a positive feedback loop and begin to associate our creative practice with an enjoyable outcome.

Rewards are not the carrot on a stick

Keep in mind that this reward is never the reason why we do our creative practice. It's not a "do this and you'll get this" kind of thing. It's just a little bit of positive reinforcement for following through and doing what you said you were going to do in the first place. This is why it's important to keep these rewards small and frequent.

The reward itself can be anything that makes you happy: such as a trip to the dog park, getting your favorite drink at Starbucks, or taking a long hot bath while someone else deals with the kids.

Personally, I like to scale up my rewards. So for example, completing my daily creative practice may earn me a piece of chocolate. At the same time, doing my creative practice every day for a week straight, might earn me a trip to Starbucks. If I'm successful for 30 days in a row, maybe I'll treat myself and pick up that new book I've been wanting to read.

Keep in mind that everyone is different. You might find it helpful to sit down and brainstorm a list of potential rewards and then separate them into daily, weekly, and monthly rewards. A rewards brainstorming worksheet has also been included in the free bonus guide for this book. I would suggest simply trying out a few different rewards and see what works best for you.

PUTTING IT ALL TOGETHER

Far too often we wait for that ideal moment in our life to start our creative projects.

We decide to wait until we can attend that 2-week writer's retreat next Summer or that painting workshop in July. We wait until our lives slow down, our kids leave home, or we retire from our full-time jobs. We tell ourselves that to start any sooner is simply a waste of time.

So we put our creative life on hold, and we wait...

Creativity is a marathon, not a sprint

Sometimes as creative artists we can get locked into this idea that if we can't do everything we want to do when we want to do it, we may as well not do anything at all. If we can't quit our job and write our novel, then what's the point?

It's not just our creative projects either. This attitude of waiting until the right time often extends to other parts of our life as well. If I can't run every day, then I might as well not run at all. If I can't stick to my diet every day, then I might as well eat whatever the hell I want. If I'm never going to perform in front of an audience, then there's no reason for me to pick up that guitar to practice.

Getting partial credit

Fortunately for us, life is not usually an all-or-nothing proposition. As my daughter's Algebra teacher has pointed out, it is possible to get partial credit, but only if you're willing to put in the work and try.

You don't have to have all of the right answers, but you do have to be willing to put your doubts aside and do what you can with what you have. Maybe you'll figure it out as you go along, or maybe you won't, but it doesn't really matter because you get credit for the attempt and not the final result. Partial credit is always better than none.

Doing something creates movement and momentum that will eventually lead you towards your next work. Doing something has the ability to clear out the cobwebs, break through the creative blocks, and jostle your imagination. On the other hand, doing nothing only creates more excuses and a big stinky pile of self-pity.

Maybe your creative process will never be the way you imagined it would be. Maybe you will never have that dedicated painting studio or that really awesome writing gazebo in the woods like Neil Gaiman, but that's okay because even though those things might be nice to have, that doesn't mean that you need them in order to do your creative work.

The world is filled with writers and visual artists who have nothing but time on their hands, and yet they have nothing to show for it. Just as there will always be those who can scrounge together 15 minutes in the morning, or an hour after the kids have gone to bed, and become successful because they are willing to dedicate those spare moments to their creative work.

It's about our small everyday actions.

Getting ourselves excited and constantly setting bigger goals for ourselves is not the answer. Most of us simply don't need more motivation. What we need is something that can help us to sit down and do our creative work with what little time we may have.

Creative triggers are small sparks that can help us get started. They are different for each of us, and it often takes a little experimentation to find the right combination that will help support our creative efforts.

Instead of setting ourselves up for failure with big dreams and unrealistic goals, it's often far better to establish a few easy-to-do creative practices that allow us to frequently taste success.

In the end, it's not so much about doing big things, as it is about just sitting down and doing something. What we repeatedly do, is what we become. As the writer Annie Dillard once said, "How we spend our days is how we spend our lives."

Choose wisely.

BONUS GUIDE & WORKSHEETS

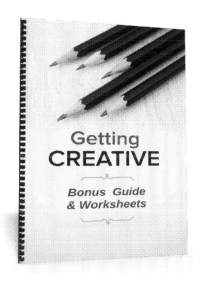

I know that we've covered a lot of information in this book about creative habits and practices, and sometimes it's hard to remember everything and put these things into action.

That's why I created a free bonus guide for this book that includes all of the worksheets, logs, and online resources that can help you to pull all of this information together.

Inside, you'll find a copy of the Creativity Log that we talked about in the book, a Creative Practice checklist, an accountability worksheet, and rewards list, along with a few additional tips and suggestions for designing your own creative practices. Also, I recommend some free tools and online resources that might help you along the way.

We'll also be able to keep in touch, talk about what's on your mind, and you'll be among the first to know when future books are released at a special discount. To download your free copy of the "Getting Creative: Bonus Guide & Worksheets" simply visit: **http://gettingcreativebook.com/bonus**

ABOUT THE AUTHOR

Drew is a writer, teacher, and head custodian of the Skinny Artist online creative community. He can often be found wandering about online, drinking lukewarm coffee, and avoiding any type of productive activity.

Writing long rambling books is only a small part of what I do. The rest of my time is spent writing long rambling blog posts, watching funny cat videos, yelling at small children (mostly my own), overfeeding our fat brown dog, and encouraging other creative souls to live their art.

If you would like to share your thoughts, ask me a question, or simply say hello—I would love to hear from you. Take a minute and drop me a line at drew@skinnycatstudios.com

If you would like to hang out, here's how we can connect:

Creative ranting website: SkinnyArtist.com
Publishing website: SkinnyCatStudios.com
Facebook: https://www.facebook.com/LiveYourArt
Twitter: @SkinnyArtist
YouTube: https://www.youtube.com/user/SkinnyFlicks